I HOPE YOU DANCE

JOURNAL

MARK D. SANDERS & TIA SILLERS

THOMAS NELSON
Since 1798

NASHVILLE DALLAS MEXICO CITY RIO DE JANEIRO BEIJING

PERSONALIZE THIS JOURNAL
With your own photograph

Simply attach the photo corners.
(in the envelope at the back of the journal)
to the first page in the
appropriate position so that your
own photograph
shows through
the window in the front cover.

ISBN-10: 1-4016-0030-1
ISBN-13: 978-1-4016-0030-3
PRINTED IN CHINA
11 — 09 08 07

I Hope You Dance

I hope you never lose your sense of wonder
You get your fill to eat but always keep that hunger
May you never take one single breath for granted
God forbid love ever leave you empty-handed
I hope you still feel small when you stand beside the ocean
Whenever one door closes I hope one more opens
Promise me that you'll give faith a fighting chance
And when you get the choice to sit it out or dance
I hope you dance...I hope you dance

> I hope you never fear those mountains in the distance
> Never settle for the path of least resistance
> Livin' might mean takin' chances but they're worth takin'
> Lovin' might be a mistake but it's worth makin'
> Don't let some hell-bent heart leave you bitter
> When you come close to sellin' out reconsider
> Give the heavens above more than just a passing glance
> And when you get the chance to sit it out or dance
> I hope you dance...I hope you dance

Time is a wheel in constant motion always rolling us along
Tell me who wants to look back on their years and wonder
Where those years have gone
I hope you dance...I hope you dance
I hope you dance

Oh no.

YOU KNOW WHAT THIS IS,
DON'T YOU?
IT'S A JOURNAL. FLIP OVER TO
THE NEXT PAGE AND
TELL ME WHAT YOU SEE.
NOTHING, RIGHT?
JUST A BUNCH OF BLANK PAGES WAITING
FOR YOU.

This is a journal for your journey, and how you are going to fill it is one big mystery. The words haven't come yet. Maybe the story hasn't happened. What are you going to say? Where are you going to start? How are you going to feel? Embarrassed? Will you ever let someone else read what you've written? You don't have to decide right now. There are 144 blank pages from here to the end of the book. And that's just this book. Who knows how many more of these books are meant to be in your life.

There are some people in this world who wouldn't know what to do with all this space. But that's not you. And there are some people who wouldn't want to reveal or dig down deep or talk about what scares them. But that's not you either. You're a dancer. You know that time is a wheel in constant motion. And you know if you ever start to wonder where those years have gone, all you'll have to do is open this book.

You really don't have to be so careful of what you write. Maybe someday some unborn grandchildren will find this book in a box in a trunk in an attic. Maybe they'll see that you weren't perfect . . . and love you more for it. Maybe they'll discover some secrets . . . and feel closer to you. Maybe they'll feel a little more related, understand themselves a little more, know where they're going just a little better. Is that so bad?

No, no, and no! And please don't tell me you'll start tomorrow. Pick up a permanent pen (pencils have erasers—your life doesn't) right now and repeat after me . . .

By the powers vested in me by me I say,

" Brain, start your engines!

Nonbelievers, shut your yaps!

Ready or not, here I write."

Dear Jenn,

    I know that I was supposed to mail your letter to your house since I'm a dolt but I thought it would be cute to give it to you as a present ☺. You are a huge inspiration to me and the best friend I have. You're beautiful in every way! I hope your affirmation classes helped you renew your faith in God, and will inspire others to do the same. I'm so glad to be your friend and have you in my life. I love you!

Love Always
Nahi
XOXO

It's my turn again.

Don't worry. I haven't read what you've written.
I'm just here to ask how deep you've been digging,
if you're finding treasures that prove you're alive
and human like the rest of us. I hope you've been
asking the questions and not expecting the answers.
In a word (or fourteen) I hope you've been
thinking and thriving, wondering, trusting, crying,
laughing, offering, yearning. Yeah, and dancing.

AND I HOPE life's been treating you fair, although it surely doesn't have to. And if it hasn't, I hope you've been writing down those troubles and travails. Because if you deny or hide or stuff all those sharp edges down inside, they're just going to keep cutting.

But if you deal (some might say duel) with them, and put them in their place, and tell them,

"You are not going to haunt me," they'll give up. Troubles are stubborn, but you must be a little stubborn too or else you wouldn't still be here.

That's why I like you.

Let's talk about mountains. You start climbing one, you toil, you sweat, you finally reach the top, and what do you get? Well, along with a sense of accomplishment, of peace, of a job well done, along with the satisfaction of doing what you set out to do . . . you get a great view of the next mountain. Looming. Challenging. Calling your name.

But wait! Don't feel like you have to take on that next mountain yet. Let's dwell on this one for a while. Lay there with your hands stretched out behind your head. Watch the clouds running across the sky and tell yourself you're on top of the world because in a sense you are. Just be for now, for you. Then, when you're ready . . . pick yourself up, dust yourself off, put that pack on your back, and start climbing down. One foot in front of the other, that's all you can do. This walk never ends, you know. There's always another mountain. That's what makes life thrilling and you breathless.

There are days, there are times, when you feel like you've walked so far, when the voice inside you is complaining that it's all uphill, that it always will be. And then, after all that, way beyond your blue horizon, you see the biggest mountains you've ever seen, and you think, "I can't do that."

Well, I hope you always have somebody who tells you that you can. Like I'm telling you now.

You know, I don't have any more answers than you have. I waited until the end to tell you that. I'm as scared as you are of just going through the motions in life, of not getting anywhere. All I know is that time really is a wheel in constant motion, always rolling us along. Raise your hand if you want to look back on your years and wonder where those years have gone. You have to carpe the diem. You have to seize the day. That is what I hope for you, as you live and as you love and as you fill up these pages with your story. And it doesn't matter if it's good enough for anyone else to read. That's why it's called YOUR story.

Will you promise me something?

When you do get to the last page of this book, don't
stop. No, don't stop there. Think of it as one of
those mountains. Bask in your accomplishment for a
little bit. Look back on all you've been through . . .
on all you've survived. Than make yourself go out and
get another book, another blank book, another
do-it-yourself mountain.

And write about your dance.

You do know you're a great dancer,
don't you?